SHEFFIELD BUSES

KEITH A. JENKINSON

AMBERLEY

First published 2023

Amberley Publishing
The Hill, Stroud
Gloucestershire, GL5 4EP

www.amberley-books.com

Copyright © Keith A. Jenkinson, 2023

The right of Keith A. Jenkinson to be identified
as the Author of this work has been asserted in
accordance with the Copyrights, Designs and
Patents Act 1988.

ISBN 978 1 3981 0954 4 (print)
ISBN 978 1 3981 0955 1 (ebook)

British Library Cataloguing in Publication Data.
A catalogue record for this book is available from
the British Library.

Origination by Amberley Publishing.
Printed in the UK.

Introduction

Known as the 'Steel City' due to its numerous metalworks, Sheffield is the largest city in South Yorkshire, with a population in excess of 551,000 and bordered to the south by the picturesque Derbyshire Dales. Until 1 April 1974 when South Yorkshire PTE was created by the merging of the municipal bus operations of Sheffield, Rotherham and Doncaster, Sheffield (Corporation) Transport provided most of the local transport services in the city, with other operators such as Chesterfield (Corporation) Transport, East Midland Motor Services, Yorkshire Traction and West Riding/Yorkshire Woollen District providing the longer distance services along with a tiny handful of independent companies. Then, after acquiring several Doncaster area independents, in August 1975 the PTE gained further strength when it purchased old established Sheffield independent Booth & Fisher of Halfway and in 1981 acquired Phillipson of Goldthorpe, who traded as Dearnways. The PTE used the fleet name South Yorkshire Transport and adopted a new cream and coffee livery, and in 1986 became an arms-length company using the same title, but in 1989 changed its identity to Mainline and its livery to yellow and red for Sheffield and yellow and blue for Rotherham. Then, in November 1993 the PTE sold its bus and coach operation to its management and soon afterwards Stagecoach took a 20 per cent stake in the new company. This, however, fell foul of the Office of Fair Trading, and as a consequence Stagecoach sold its holding to First Group in January 1996. Following this, First purchased the remaining 80 per cent in 1998 and in 2000 changed the company's title from First Mainline to First South Yorkshire. Looking back to 1979, Sheffield became the first place in the UK to operate bendibuses when it hired five Leyland-DABs and five MAN SG192s, which the PTE used until 1982, and then in 1985 it purchased thirteen Leyland-DABs, which it operated until 1999.

Upon the deregulation of local bus services in October 1986, the doorway was opened to several independent operators who began to compete with the PTE. Among the first were Andrews, who had started life in 1982 as a HGV and PSV driving school; Mike Groves; Richardson, who had begun as a coach operator in 1976; SUT, who started as Trushelfco (No. 1019) in November 1986 and was branded as NTE Coaches before becoming SUT in March 1987; and already established Dinnington-based Excelsior. Of these, Andrews was taken over by Yorkshire Traction in 1992, Excelsior was acquired by SUT in 1987, and Groves and Richardson were purchased by SYT in 1989. Then, old established Wigmores of Dinnington changed ownership and morphed into Northern Bus before ultimately becoming MAS Special Engineering and then BrightBus until July 2017 when it closed due to the failing health of its owner.

Seeing the success of those who had taken the plunge in the early days of deregulation led others to enter the fray, and in 1988 Sheaf Line and Yorkshire Terrier made their appearance using Leyland Nationals while Compass Buses, who used the fleet name Sheffield & District Traction Co. and was an offshoot of West Riding Automobile Company, also made its debut in the city. Then, seeking to expand, Yorkshire Terrier took over the remains of Darley Dale independent Woolliscroft (Silver Service) and renamed it Kingsman. After only eight months, however, Sheaf Line was taken over by SUT and was then sold to Mainline in September 1994, Yorkshire Terrier/Kingsman was acquired by Yorkshire Traction in 1995, and Compass Buses sold its Sheffield & District operation to South Yorkshire Transport (former PTE) in September 1989 but retained its services in Wakefield and Leeds. Meanwhile, in 1989 Stagecoach had acquired East Midland Motor Services, who already operated into Sheffield on services from Chesterfield and Nottingham, and then in July 1995 purchased the former municipal bus operator Chesterfield Transport.

Continuing the flow of new independent operators in Sheffield, in August 1990 Basichour, who traded as Sheffield Omnibus, was inaugurated and launched itself in the city with some ex-Preston Corporation Leyland Atlanteans. At the start of the following year a new minibus operator – Don Valley Bus Services – appeared on the scene, and in July 1992 South Riding was born, using Leyland Nationals. Moving forward, South Riding and Basichour (Sheffield Omnibus) were both sold to Yorkshire Traction, in 1994 and 1995 respectively, whereas Don Valley Buses had passed to Mainline in June 1993.

On 31 March 1994, trams were reintroduced to Sheffield – the last ones had operated on 8 October 1960. This time they were in the form of three module articulated single deckers owned and operated by South Yorkshire PTE. After extending the new system to four lines but suffering operational and management problems, South Yorkshire Supertram was sold to Stagecoach in December 1997, with the PTE retaining the infrastructure and its new owner accepting responsibility for the maintenance and operation of the network until 2024.

Although by now some of the independents had disappeared, others began to try their luck on the city's streets, one of which was Dewsbury-based Yorkshire Travel, who had financial backing from Mainline in an attempt to break into the West Yorkshire bus market but also operated a service to Sheffield from Huddersfield. Then came Sheffield-based Aston Express which began operating in June 1995 and survived until August 2004 when it was acquired by Stagecoach East Midland.

Already having a small presence in Sheffield following its acquisition of East Midland Motor Services in 1989 and Chesterfield Transport in 1995, Stagecoach strengthened its position in the city when, in December 2005, it purchased Yorkshire Traction and merged together its Andrews Sheffield Omnibus and Yorkshire Terrier operations, which remained thus until 2006. Meanwhile, in 2004 Chesterfield-based independent TM Travel entered the city when it took over Thompson Travel's service from Chesterfield, and over the next few years they gained some tendered services in the city before selling to Wellglade (Trent) in January 2010. Finally (within the remit of this book), in 2007 Veolia (Dunn Line) gained a few tendered services in South Yorkshire, bringing it into the city where it remained for a few years.

In recent years, Sheffield has been dominated by the larger conglomerates such as First South Yorkshire and Stagecoach who have swept away most of the independent operators, leaving only old established Hulleys, Baslow, TM Travel (now owned by Wellglade) and Powells of Hellaby, who was acquired by HCT Group in 2017, to be regularly seen. Despite this, however, the city still provides a great deal of interest for transport enthusiasts and is well worthy of a visit.

Seen in Sheffield's Pond Street bus station is municipal-owned Sheffield Transport 308 (UWA 308L), an East Lancs-bodied Leyland AN68/1R Atlantean which was new in July 1973. (T. W. W. Knowles)

Looking superb in its owner's corporate ivory and blue livery, Sheffield Transport 773 (WWJ 773M) is a Park Royal-bodied Daimler CRG6 Fleetline, which began life in October 1973. (T. W. W. Knowles)

Heading through its home city, and followed by a Yorkshire Traction single decker, is Sheffield Transport Park Royal-bodied AEC Swift 23 (TWE 23F), which had been purchased new in June 1968. (Neil Halliday collection)

Now preserved, Northern Counties-bodied Leyland Panther ENU 93H was new to Chesterfield Corporation in September 1969. (K. A. Jenkinson)

Seen heading along Abbeydale Road, Sheffield, en route to Millhouses, is South Yorkshire Transport Van Hool McArdle-bodied Ailsa B55 403 (LWB 403P) which was new in August 1976. (K. A. Jenkinson)

Resting in Sheffield between two South Yorkshire PTE buses is East Midland Duple-bodied Leyland Leopard 17 (UAU 17S), which was new in August 1977 and is seen here in NBC livery displaying both East Midland and Mansfield District fleet names. (K. A. Jenkinson)

Wearing unrelieved NBC green livery and standing outside Sheffield railway station is East Midland Marshall-bodied Bristol RELL6L 533 (CRR 533J), which was new in September 1970. (K. A. Jenkinson)

New to Sheffield Corporation in October 1968 and seen here in South Yorkshire PTE's corporate cream and coffee livery, 605 (WWB 205G) was a dual-door Park Royal-bodied Leyland PDR2/1 Atlantean. (K. A. Jenkinson)

With two destination boxes on its cove panels is South Yorkshire PTE Park Royal-bodied AEC Swift 39 (TWE 119F), which had started life with Sheffield JOC in May 1968. (K. A. Jenkinson)

New to South Yorkshire PTE in December 1980 and wearing its corporate cream and coffee livery, Leyland National 2 31 (KWA 31W) is pictured here when only a couple of years old in Sheffield's Pond Street bus station. (K. A. Jenkinson)

A line of five South Yorkshire PTE buses rest between duties at Pond Street bus station, Sheffield. Nearest the camera are Daimler CRG6LX Fleetline 976 (AWB 976B), which was new in June 1964, and Leyland PDR2/1 Atlantean 562 (BWB 562H) which dates from October 1969, both of which have Park Royal bodies. (K. A. Jenkinson)

Painted in original Clipper livery for operation on Sheffield's city centre 500 service are two South Yorkshire Transport Leyland-DAB bendibuses headed by 2002 (C102 HDT), which entered service in August 1985. (T. M. Leach collection)

Awaiting its Castleton-bound passengers in Pond Street bus station, Sheffield, on 22 October 1992 is Hulleys of Baslow's Plaxton-bodied Leyland Leopard RVO 661L, which had been new to Trent in March 1973. (K. A. Jenkinson)

New to Yorkshire Traction in April 1979, Leyland National YWG 467T is seen here in Pond Street, Sheffield, after being acquired by local independent Andrews. (K. A. Jenkinson)

Resting in Pond Street bus station, Sheffield, is another of Andrews buses, this time ex-West Midlands PTE Park Royal-bodied Leyland FE30AGR Fleetline SDA 647S. (K. A. Jenkinson)

Awaiting its Leeds-bound passengers in Pond Street bus station, Sheffield, and displaying West Riding and Yorkshire fleet names together with an NBC logo, is Duple-bodied Leyland Leopard RYG 397R. (T. W. W. Knowles)

An early post-deregulation Sheffield independent was Groves, most of whose buses carried all-over advertising for Nu-Life Window Co. Here 1973-vintage ex-Merseyside PTE MCW-bodied Daimler CRG6 Fleetline CKC 319L is seen in the city centre. (Author's collection)

Starting life as a coach company, Richardson diversified into local bus operation soon after deregulation. Seen here on 6 May 1989 is Plaxton-bodied Leyland Leopard JDK 922P which was new to Lancashire United Transport in August 1975. (K. A. Jenkinson)

New to Merthyr Tydfill UDC in November 1973, ECW-bodied Bristol RESL6H NHB 188M is seen here with Excelsior, Dinnington, who acquired it in October 1986 and sold it with the company to SUT in February 1987. It then passed to Yelloway, Rochdale, in January 1988. Standing next to it is South Yorkshire Transport Alexander-bodied Dennis Dominator 2159 (NKU 159X). (Author's collection)

Seen here with SUT, in whose fleet it was given fleet number 25, is Leyland National OCN 232L, which started life with Northern General in July 1973. (T. M. Leach collection)

Standing in Leeds bus station awaiting its departure to Sheffield on the White Rose Express service for which it is branded is West Riding Willowbrook-bodied Leyland Leopard 21 (PUB 67W). (Barry Newsome collection)

New to Trent, Northern Bus ECW-bodied Bristol VRT 3028 (URB 828S) is seen here fitted with a cast fleet number plate and immaculately presented like the rest of its owner's fleet. (T. S. Blackman)

Leaving Meadowhall (Sheffield) bus station on an X60 journey on 25 April 1998 is Northern Bus ex-City of Oxford Duple-bodied Leyland Tiger 1310 (EBW 100Y). (K. A. Jenkinson)

Seen approaching Sheffield Pond Street bus station is pristinely presented Northern Bus Leyland National 2879 (YFB 970V), which started life with Bristol Omnibus Company in December 1979. (K. A. Jenkinson)

For a few months, Stagecoach Cleveland Transit (Hull) operated bendibuses on its long 909 service from Sheffield to Grimsby. Here Plaxton-bodied Volvo B10MA 97 (T97 JHN) is seen in July 1999 adorned with appropriate branding for the service. (R. G. Pope)

Awaiting its passengers in Pond Street bus station, Sheffield, in January 1994 is Sheaf Line's ex-Crosville Leyland National 820 (LMA 414T), behind which is a Rotherham Mainline-liveried Alexander-bodied Dennis Dominator. (K. A. Jenkinson)

Also seen in January 1994, albeit in a reverse livery to that in the previous photograph, is Sheaf Line Leyland National 825 (GUB 178N), which began life with Yorkshire Woollen District Transport in October 1974. (K. A. Jenkinson)

Seen exiting Pond Street bus station, Sheffield, on 22 October 1992 is Kingsman Travel Leyland National 62 (BCD 822L), which was new to Southdown in June 1973 and had later operated for Top Line on whose livery it is based here. (K. A. Jenkinson)

Coming out of Haymarket, Sheffield, on 22 October 1992 is Yorkshire Terrier Leyland National 35 (NWT 715M), which started life with York West Yorkshire in December 1973. (K. A. Jenkinson)

About to cross two counties after leaving South Yorkshire, Hanley-bound passengers board PMT's ex-Crosville Duple-bodied Leyland Leopard 2336 (JMB 336T) in Pond Street bus station, Sheffield, in October 1991. (P. French)

New to Northern General but seen here after being acquired by Compass Buses (Sheffield & District) is Leyland National 92 (MCN 832L), which began life in December 1972. (Campbell Morrison)

Sheffield & District Leyland Lynx 253 (D204 FBK) is seen here still wearing the livery of Hants & Sussex, to whom it was new in December 1986. (Campbell Morriston)

About to leave Pond Street bus station, Sheffield, on a journey to Woodhouse is Sheffield & District Leyland Lynx 262 (E262 TUB), which was new in January 1988. (Campbell Morrison)

New to East Midland in January 1983 and seen here after its acquisition by Stagecoach whose original striped livery it wears as it stands in Pond Street bus station, Sheffield, in April 1995, is ECW-bodied Leyland Tiger 31 (SKY 31Y). (K. A. Jenkinson)

Seen in Sheffield's Pond Street bus station in October 1993 is Stagecoach subsidiary East Midland's Alexander (Belfast)-bodied Mercedes Benz 709D 745 (L745 LWA), which was new in September 1993. (K. A. Jenkinson)

New to Stagecoach East Midland in July 1993, and seen here in Pond Street bus interchange, Sheffield, in October of that year is Northern Counties Volvo Olympian 103 (K103 JWJ). (K. A. Jenkinson)

In use as a driver trainer by South Yorkshire Transport is Park Royal-bodied Daimler CRG6LXB M106 (WWJ 761M), which had been purchased new by SYPTE in October 1973. (K. S. E. Till)

Still painted in its latest SYT livery but having gained new Mainline vinyls on its lower panels, Alexander-bodied Dennis Dominator 2128 (KKU 218W), which was new in June 1981, is seen here in Pond Street bus station, Sheffield, in January 1994. (K. A. Jenkinson)

Also in Pond Street bus station, Sheffield, in January 1994, and still in SYT livery (to which a Mainline fleet name has been added) is coach-seated Alexander-bodied Dennis Dominator 2490 (D490 OWE), which dates from October 1986. (K. A. Jenkinson)

Painted in South Yorkshire Transport's then current livery with recently added Mainline fleet names and seen here leaving Meadowhall bus station, Sheffield, on 28 April 1995 is coach-seated MCW Metrobus 1941 (B941 FET). (K. A. Jenkinson)

Wearing Mainline's Rotherham district colours, South Yorkshire Transport Leyland-DAB bendibus 2013 (C113 HDT) is seen here in Sheffield en route to Crystal Peaks. (Author's collection)

Standing in Pond Street bus station, Sheffield, adorned in Rotherham Mainline livery, Alexander-bodied Dennis Dominator 2179 (NKU 179X) awaits departure to its home town on 3 April 1993. (K. A. Jenkinson)

Seen leaving Meadowhall bus station in May 1998, branded for route 41 is Mainline Alexander PS-bodied Volvo B10M 736 (M736 VET), which was new in June 1995. (K. A. Jenkinson)

Another Mainline Alexander PS-bodied Volvo B10M pictured leaving Meadowhall bus station in May 1998 is 745 (N745 CKY), which is branded for the X78 service from Sheffield to Doncaster. (K. A. Jenkinson)

Continuing Mainline's route branding purge, this time for the 52, 1990 vintage Alexander PS-bodied Volvo B10M 604 (G604 NWA) is also seen departing from Meadowhall bus station in May 1998. (K. A. Jenkinson)

Another bus seen exiting from Meadowhall bus station in May 1998 is Rotherham Mainline-liveried Alexander PS-bodied Volvo B10M 662 (H662 THL), which was new in May 1991. (K. A. Jenkinson)

Collecting its passengers in Pond Street bus station, Sheffield, in September 1998 is Hulleys of Baslow's Leyland National RRA 218X, which began life with Trent in November 1981. (K. A. Jenkinson)

Standing at their depot on 9 September 2000 are Powell Bus of Hellaby's ex-Lothian ECW-bodied Leyland Olympian 680 (OFS 680Y) and former Eastern National Leyland National DAR 128T. (K. A. Jenkinson)

Displaying WYPTE and NBC logos below its windscreen and sporting a Metro Coach fleet name on its side panels, West Yorkshire PTE Plaxton-bodied Leyland Leopard 1531 (JUM 531V) leaves Pond Street bus station, Sheffield, at the start of its journey to Huddersfield. (Author's collection)

Seen leaving Meadowhall bus station in May 1998 when only a few days old is Mainline's Plaxton Beaver-bodied Mercedes Benz 0814D 136 (R136 XDT). (K. A. Jenkinson)

Departing from Meadowhall bus station on a 143 journey to Rotherham is Mainline's Plaxton-bodied Volvo B6 428 (M428 VHE), which except for its front was covered in a contravision all-over advert. (K. A. Jenkinson)

Squeezing into Pond Street bus station, Sheffield, in September 1998 is First PMT Jonckheere Jubilee-bodied Volvo B10M SBV883 (TJI 4828), which began life in February 1989 with Berks Bucks (Bee Line) registered F758 OJH. (K. A. Jenkinson)

With a Northern Bus Express fleet name on its upper side panels is immaculately presented ECW-bodied Bristol VRT 3034 (RMA 434V), which started life with Crosville in March 1980. (T. S. Blackman)

New to SELNEC PTE in December 1972, Park Royal-bodied Leyland AN68/1R Atlantean WBN 979L is seen here in Sheffield city centre on 3 January 1989 after being purchased by Sheaf Line in whose fleet it was numbered 9. (S. K. Jenkinson)

Making its way through Sheffield city centre is local independent Andrews Northern Counties low-height-bodied Daimler CRG6 Fleetline 1703 (LDC 81P), which started life with Cleveland Transit in March 1976. (P. T. Stokes)

Resting in Pond Street bus station, Sheffield, before undertaking a journey to Hanley is First PMT Optare Delta-bodied DAF SB220 SAD802 (H802 GRE), which was new in August 1990. (K. A. Jenkinson)

Starting life with Chesterfield Corporation in July 1980, but seen here at Sheffield's Meadowhall shopping centre coach park after passing to Stagecoach East Midland, is Leyland National 2 28 (EKY 28V). (K. A. Jenkinson)

Devoid of all graphics except for fleet number 93 is Sheffield & District Leyland National FHE 401L, which was new to Yorkshire Traction in January 1973. (Author's collection)

Seen here in Pond Street bus station, Sheffield, wearing Budget Bus livery for the 25 and 25A services, is Mainline Alexander-bodied Dennis Dominator 2194 (NKU 194X). (K. A. Jenkinson)

Pictured on 16 February 1997 sporting The Eyrie Experience branding on its side panels is Mainline Duple-bodied Leyland Tiger 1001 (TPD 126Y), which had started life with London Country in May 1983. (Barry Newsome)

Resting in Pond Street bus station, Sheffield, in October 1989 is Kingsman Travel Leyland National 63 (JNA 589N), which was new to Greater Manchester PTE in May 1983. (K. A. Jenkinson)

Seen in Sheffield looking freshly repainted in October 1996 is Yorkshire Traction subsidiary Andrews Sheffield Omnibus former West Midlands PTE MCW-bodied Leyland FE30ALR Fleetline 1726 (NOC 420R). (P. T. Stokes)

New to SUT in October 1987, Neoplan N416 101 (E101 VWA) is seen in Sheffield city centre on 3 April 1993 after passing to Sheaf Line. About to overtake it is South Riding's ex-United Leyland National 14 (JBR 688T). (K. A. Jenkinson)

Leaving Meadowhall bus station, Sheffield, on the 293 service to Rawmarsh on 14 May 1998 is Thompson Travel's Duple-bodied Leyland Leopard MPL 133W, which began life with London Country in June 1981. (K. A. Jenkinson)

Resting in Pond Street bus station, Sheffield, in September 1998 is Northern Bus ECW-bodied Leyland Tiger TPD 105X, which had been fitted with a new front by East Lancs coachbuilders but had been new to London Country in July 1982. (K. A. Jenkinson)

Departing from Meadowhall bus station, Sheffield, on the M1 service to its home town on 14 May 1998, is First Huddersfield Plaxton-bodied Dennis Lance 4014 (M414 VWW). (K. A. Jenkinson)

Seen in Pond Street bus station, Sheffield, in 1995 wearing Bradfield Bus livery is Northern Bus ECW-bodied Bristol VRT 3076 (XRR 176S), which had started life with East Midland in June 1978. (Campbell Morrison)

New to Yorkshire Woollen District in February 1977, Leyland National TUG 809R was then operated by Sheaf Line before passing in September 1994 to Mainline with whom it is seen here at Meadowhall bus station numbered 813. (Campbell Morrison)

Leaving Meadowhall bus station on its journey from Sheffield to Barnsley on 22 October 1992 is Yorkshire Traction ECW-bodied Leyland Olympian 656 (A656 OCX), which began its life with its subsidiary, County Motors. (K. A. Jenkinson)

Seen exiting Meadowhall bus station on 14 May 1998 is Mainline towing vehicle 9004 (OWJ 354A), which had been converted from Doncaster Corporation 1962 vintage Roe-bodied Leyland PD3/4 476 HDT. (K. A. Jenkinson)

Sheffield Buses

Fitted with guide wheels for guided busways experiments on a test track constructed at Mainline's Rotherham depot (which came to nothing), MCW Metrobus 1894, which was new in March 1981 and registered JHE 194W, is seen here on 3 April 1993 sporting a dummy SYT number plate. (K. A. Jenkinson)

Resting on Meadowhall shopping complex car park on 27 October 2001 is Stagecoach East Midland Plaxton-bodied Volvo B10M 641 (L641 LDT). (K. A. Jenkinson)

Pictured in Pond Street bus station, Sheffield, in 1994 is SUT-owned Sheaf Line Leyland National 11 (NOE 595R), which began life with Midland Red in April 1977 and was converted to Greenway specification by East Lancs Coachbuilders in October 1992. (Barry Newsome)

Resting between duties in Sheffield's Pond Street bus interchange in October 1998 is Yorkshire Travel Leyland National 2 21 (YPL 383T), which started life with London Country in October 1978. (K. A. Jenkinson)

Collecting its passengers in Pond Street, Sheffield, outside the bus station is South Riding's ex-Crosville Leyland National 18 (RFM 893M). (K. A. Jenkinson)

Leaving Meadowhall bus station on the 747 service to Chesterfield on 28 April 1998 is Stagecoach East Midland Alexander-bodied Leyland Tiger 429 (B629 DWF). (K. A. Jenkinson)

New to Crosville in March 1978, Yorkshire Travel Leyland National 12 (CFM 349S) stands in Pond Street bus interchange, Sheffield, awaiting its departure to Huddersfield on the 239 service in September 1998. (K. A. Jenkinson)

Followed through Sheffield city centre by a Yorkshire Terrier Leyland National in 1994 is Sheffield Omnibus dual-door East Lancs-bodied Leyland AN68A Atlantean CRN 125S, which had been acquired from Preston Bus to whom it had been new in December 1977. (K. A. Jenkinson)

Seen in Meadowhall bus station in 1994 is Sheffield Omnibus Alexander-bodied Volvo B6R 2273 (K273 ERM), which had started life with Stagecoach Cumberland in November 1992. (Campbell Morrison)

Seen approaching Meadowhall bus station in 1992, Barnsley & District ECW-bodied Bristol VRT HWE 826N began life with its parent Yorkshire Traction in March 1975. Later passing to Johnson, Hodthorpe, in August 1993, it was exported to Holland as a non-PSV in 2011. (K. A. Jenkinson)

Leaving Meadowhall bus station on 14 May 1998 is Mainline MCW Metrorider 3003 (D644 MDB), which was new to GM Buses in April 1987. (K. A. Jenkinson)

Seen outside SUT's Charlotte Road depot, Sheffield, on 5 May 1992 with another Sheaf Line Leyland National and a Don Valley Buses minibus is 124 (CWX 664T), which began life with West Riding in January 1979. (K. A. Jenkinson)

Yorkshire Traction subsidiary Barnsley & District's Leyland National SWE 437S, which was new to its parent company in August 1977, is seen here approaching Sheffield's Pond Street bus station in September 1998. (K. A. Jenkinson)

Starting life with London Country in May 1983 and seen here at SUT's Charlotte Road, Sheffield, depot on 7 December 1991 displaying Sheaf Line and Premier Coachline fleet names is Duple-bodied Leyland Tiger 1001 (YPD 126Y). (K. A. Jenkinson)

Seen in Pond Street bus interchange, Sheffield, in October 1998 is Stagecoach East Midland Alexander-bodied Volvo Olympian 145 (P145 KWJ) adorned with adverts at each side of its destination screen. (K. A. Jenkinson)

Standing in Sheffield's Pond Street bus station wearing National Express 'Shuttle' and route branding and awaiting its departure to Leeds is Yorkshire Rider Plaxton-bodied Volvo B10M 1426 (L546 XUT), which was new in July 1994. (K. A. Jenkinson)

New to Nottingham City Transport in April 1994, Yorkshire Terrier Alexander-bodied Volvo B6 2226 (L501 OAL) is seen here at its owner's Ecclesfield depot on 27 October 2001. (K. A. Jenkinson)

With a paper label in its windscreen lettered 'Hathersage', Stagecoach East Midland Reeve Burgess-bodied Mercedes Benz 811D 722 (G822 KWF) rests in Pond Street bus station, Sheffield, in August 1998. (K. A. Jenkinson)

West Riding Wright-bodied Volvo B10B 407 (L407 NUA), which was new to the company in October 1993, stands in Pond Street bus station, Sheffield, awaiting its departure to Bradford on 20 January 1995. (K. A. Jenkinson)

Seen on 3 April 1993 in Pond Street bus station, Sheffield, is Yorkshire Traction's eight-year old, coach-seated ECW-bodied Leyland Olympian 668 (B668 EWE), which is freshly repainted and carries branding for the Fastlink service to Leeds. (K. A. Jenkinson)

New to PMT in August 1975 and seen here in Pond Street bus station, Sheffield, on 20 January 1995 after its acquisition by South Riding, is Leyland National 16 (KRE 276P). (K. A. Jenkinson)

Painted in its original unrelieved grey livery, South Yorkshire Supertram 21 passes Sheffield Omnibus ex-Barrow Borough Transport Northern Counties-bodied Leyland AN68D/1R Atlantean LEO 734Y in Sheffield city centre on 27 April 1995. (T. S. Blackman)

Wearing Barnsley's Town Link branding, Yorkshire Traction MCW Metrorider 546 (E546 VKY), which had been purchased new in October 1987, is seen here in Sheffield's Pond Street bus station in January 1994. (K. A. Jenkinson)

New to Eastern Counties in April 1981, freshly repainted in Barnsley & District's new livery, Leyland National 2 PEX 622W is seen here leaving Meadowhall bus station on 14 May 1998. (K. A. Jenkinson)

Purchased new by Andrews, Sheffield, in May 2000 and seen here in October 2001 with Yorkshire Terrier after the two companies were merged under Yorkshire Traction ownership is East Lancs-bodied DAF SB220 2477 (W477 MKU). (K. A. Jenkinson)

With Tinsley power station's now demolished cooling towers and the M1 motorway in the background, Northern Bus MCW Metrorider D670 NNE, which had been new to GM Buses in April 1987, stands on Meadowhall shopping complex's coach park on 9 September 2000. (K. A. Jenkinson)

New in May 1978 to East Staffordshire District Council as a conventional double decker, when Leyland AN68/1R Atlantean XRF 26S was purchased by Sheffield Omnibus in December 1993 it was given a new East Lancs single-deck body with which it is seen here on 28 April 1995. (T. S. Blackman)

Standing in Pond Street bus interchange, Sheffield, in September 1998, hiding a First Mainline Leyland-DAB bendibus is Aston Express Optare-bodied Mercedes Benz 811D F39 CWY, which was new to London Buses in March 1989. (K. A. Jenkinson)

Hulleys of Baslow ECW-bodied Leyland FE30ALR Fleetline 20 (SCH 117X), seen here at Meadowhall shopping centre car park on 25 April 1998, was new to South Notts in December 1981. (K. A. Jenkinson)

Starting life as a Dormobile demonstrator in December 1989, Don Valley Buses Mercedes Benz 811D 60 (G590 PKL) is pictured here making its way through Sheffield's Pond Street bus station in January 1994. (Barry Newsome)

Branded for the X33 service from Bradford to Sheffield, Arriva Yorkshire Wright-bodied Volvo B10B 406 (L406 NUA) is seen leaving Meadowhall bus station in October 1998. (K. A. Jenkinson)

Parked between duties in Sheffield Pond Street bus station on 22 October 1992 is Don Valley Buses Reeve Burgess-bodied Dodge S56 29 (D129 OWG), which began life with South Yorkshire Transport in February 1987. (K. A. Jenkinson)

Pictured in the Steel City on 3 April 1993, Sheffield Omnibus Alexander-bodied Bristol VRT 1538 (VRP 38S), which was new to Northampton Corporation in December 1977, carries a Nottingham Omnibus fleet name in preparation for its transfer south to Sheffield Omnibus's sister company. (K. A. Jenkinson)

Wearing National Express Rapide livery, Northumbria Bova FHD12 140 (M122 UUB) exits Meadowhall bus station on 14 May 1998 on the 326 service to Luton. (K. A. Jenkinson)

Passing beneath the raised M1 motorway soon after leaving its Meadowhall terminus on 4 May 1998 is Sheffield Supertram 18. (K. A. Jenkinson)

New to Greater Manchester PTE in June 1976 registered LJA 643P, this Northern Counties-bodied Leyland AN68A/1R Atlantean later passed to Hyndburn Transport, who re-registered it IIL 2503. Here it is seen on 3 April 1993 after being acquired by Sheffield Omnibus still wearing Hyndburn livery albeit with its front repainted into its new owner's colours. (K. A. Jenkinson)

Freshly repainted into Stagecoach livery, Supertram 107 passes below the Tinsley flyover section of the elevated M1 motorway on 4 May 1998. (K. A. Jenkinson)

Wearing Andrews livery but with part of Yorkshire Traction subsidiary's Barnsley & District fleet name in its lower windscreen, MCW Metrobus NOC 420R, which had been new to West Midlands PTE in December 1976, is seen here at Pond Street bus station, Sheffield, in January 1993 on the X10 service to Barnsley for which it has a fixed destination screen. (K. A. Jenkinson)

Approaching Meadowhall on the X10 service to its home town is Yorkshire Traction subsidiary Barnsley & District Plaxton-bodied Leyland Tiger A128 EPA, which began life with London Country. (K. A. Jenkinson)

Andrews Sheffield Omnibus ex-West Midlands PTE MCW Metrobus 1731 (KJW 304W) and former PMT Leyland National 2 2091 (A304 JFA) stand at their Ecclesfield depot on 27 October 2001. (K. A. Jenkinson)

Still wearing the livery of its previous owner, Northampton Transport, albeit with its front repainted into the colours of its new owner, Sheffield Omnibus, Alexander-bodied Bristol VRT VVV 62S is seen here in its new home city in October 1992. (K. A. Jenkinson)

Seen in Sheffield city centre on 3 April 1993 is Mainline Plaxton-bodied Volvo B6 401 (K401 EDT), which was new to South Yorkshire Transport in December 1992. (K. A. Jenkinson)

New to Eastern Counties in April 1981, Andrews Sheffield Omnibus Leyland National 2 PEX 619W is seen in the yard of its Ecclesfield depot on 27 October 2001. (K. A. Jenkinson)

Caught by the camera in Pond Street, Sheffield, is Sheffield Omnibus East Lancs-bodied Leyland Olympian A278 ROW, which was new to Southampton City Transport in March 1984. (K. A. Jenkinson)

Painted in Mainline livery but displaying a Don Valley Buses fleet name, Alexander-bodied Mercedes Benz 811D 70 (F70 LAL), which was new in May 1989 to Skills, Nottingham, is seen here at Mainline's now-closed Herries Road depot, Sheffield, on 16 February 1997. (K. A. Jenkinson)

Still wearing the livery of its former owner, Brighton Borough Transport, Sheffield Omnibus East Lancs-bodied Leyland AN68/1R Atlantean OYJ 71R is pictured here leaving Meadowhall bus station on 22 October 1992. (K. A. Jenkinson)

First Mainline MCW Mk II Metrobus 1912 (A112 XWE), which was new in September 1983, is seen here in Pond Street bus station, Sheffield, in September 1998. (K. A. Jenkinson)

A pair of Leyland National 2s – Yorkshire Terrier's ex-Yorkshire Traction EDT 219V stands alongside Andrews former Eastern Counties PEX 619W in the yard of their joint Ecclesfield depot on 27 October 2001. (K. A. Jenkinson)

New to South Yorkshire PTE in February 1981, Rolls-Royce-engined MCW Metrobus 1861 (JHE 161W), seen here in Pond Street bus station, Sheffield, in September 1998 wearing First Mainline livery, has since been preserved. (K. A. Jenkinson)

Pictured at Yorkshire Terrier's Ecclesfield depot on 27 October 2001, MCW Metrobus 1737 (POG 595Y) had been new to West Midlands PTE in January 1983. (K. A. Jenkinson)

Much travelled Park Royal-bodied Leyland Titan GNF6V, which was new to Greater Manchester PTE in November 1979, eventually found its way to Martins Coaches, Chapeltown, Sheffield, where it is seen here in April 2000 after operating a schools duty. (K. A. Jenkinson)

Parked in Sheffield's Pond Street bus interchange in April 1999 wearing branding for Meadowhall's Shuttle service is First Mainline Leyland-DAB bendibus 2003 (C103 HDT). (K. A. Jenkinson)

Seen in Pond Street bus interchange in October 1998 with 'easiaccess' lettering on its side panels is First Mainline Wright-bodied Volvo B10BLE 784 (R784 WKW), which had been purchased new by its predecessor in December 1997. (K. A. Jenkinson)

Purchased new by Andrews in May 1999 but seen here at their joint Ecclesfield depot on 27 October 2001 after passing to Yorkshire Terrier, both of whom are subsidiaries of Yorkshire Traction, is East Lancs-bodied Dennis Dart SLF142 (T142 JKY). (K. A. Jenkinson)

Starting life with South Yorkshire Transport in August 1982, First Mainline Alexander-bodied Dennis Dominator 2224 (SDT 224Y) is seen here with an advert at one side of its front destination screen. (K. A. Jenkinson)

Bought new by Sheffield Omnibus in September 1993, Alexander-bodied Leyland Olympian 1602 (L602 NOS) is seen here in Sheffield city centre on 28 April 1995. (T. S. Blackman)

Resting in the depot yard of MASS, North Anston, on 9 September 2000, are preserved ECW-bodied Bristol VRT UVT 49X and ex-Yorkshire Traction XAK 908T. UVT 49X was the last Bristol VRT to be built and was new to Stevensons, Spath, in October 1981 and later operated with Midland Fox and Crosville Wales. Several years after this photograph was taken, it was sadly stolen and never recovered, and is presumed to have been scrapped. (K. A. Jenkinson)

Departing from Meadowhall bus station in October 1998 is Andrews Sheffield Omnibus Leyland National MTJ 769S, which began life with Merseyside PTE in August 1977. (K. A. Jenkinson)

During the summer of 2000, MASS Transit purchased a sizeable number of former London Buses Leyland Titans for operation on its numerous schools services. Seen on 9 September of that year, still in their previous owners colours, are A951 SYE and NUW 627Y. (K. A. Jenkinson)

Having been repainted into the livery of their new owner, MASS Transit, former London Leyland Titans CUL 74V, which was new in September 1979, and NUW 637Y, which dated from November 1982, are seen here at their depot on 9 September 2000. (K. A. Jenkinson)

Seen at its depot on 9 September 2000 wearing London Red, Leyland Titan CUL 175V stands alongside ex-First Mainline Alexander-bodied Dennis Dominator NKU 193X, which is still in its previous operator's livery but has received MASS fleet names. (K. A. Jenkinson)

Freshly repainted into MASS Transit livery, former First Mainline Alexander-bodied Dennis Dominator NKU 217X is seen here at its owner's depot on 9 September 2000. (K. A. Jenkinson)

Still in Northern Bus livery but with the name of its new owner, Mainline, in its front nearside window is Leyland National LMA 413T, which was new to Crosville in August 1979 and is seen here displaying the 2813 fleet number of its previous owner and the 27 of Mainline below its windscreen. (K. A. Jenkinson)

First Mainline Reeves Burgess-bodied Renault S56 369 (H369 UWB) is pictured here in Pond Street bus station, Sheffield, in September 1998. (K. A. Jenkinson)

Displaying easiaccess lettering and logos on its side panels, First Mainline's Olive Grove-based Wright-bodied Volvo B6LE 443 (M443 BKY) stands in rain on 16 February 1997. (K. A. Jenkinson)

Starting life with British Airways in July 1987 and seen here in Sheffield's Pond Street bus interchange with Yorkshire Terrier in October 1993, East Lancs-bodied Scania K112CRB D93 ALX was given a new body by East Lancs in January 1999 after which it continued to operate with Yorkshire Traction, and later Stagecoach Yorkshire. (K. A. Jenkinson)

Built as a demonstrator for its coachbuilder in 2000, Caetano Nimbus-bodied Dennis Dart SLF W809 VMA was originally registered REL 905. Here it is seen on loan to First South Yorkshire at Meadowhall on 9 September 2000 while operating a shuttle service to the newly opened Magna Science Adventure Centre at Rotherham. (K. A. Jenkinson)

Seen at the Magna Science Adventure Centre on 23 May 2007 at the relaunch of the Sheffield to Doncaster 78 service (for which it is branded) is First South Yorkshire's Wright-bodied Volvo B9TL 37248 (YN07 MKF). (K. A. Jenkinson)

New to Mainline in May 1995 but seen here leaving Meadowhall bus station in May 2007 painted in First South Yorkshire livery is Plaxton-bodied Volvo B6-50 40468 (M429 VHE). (K. A. Jenkinson)

Wearing First's unattractive faded livery, indicating that it is a step-entrance bus, and seen here exiting from Meadowhall bus station on 23 May 2007, is First South Yorkshire Alexander PS-bodied Volvo B10M 60595 (N758 CKY), which dated from March 1996. (K. A. Jenkinson)

Operated by Dunn Line on the tendered South Yorkshire T Travel A1 service from Sheffield to Rotherham is Optare Solo 5609 (YJ56 AUO), pictured here departing from Meadowhall bus station on 23 May 2007. (K. A. Jenkinson)

Painted in National Express corporate livery with 'Shuttle' branding is Birmingham Coach Company Van Hool-bodied Scania K124IB4 X422 WVO, which was new in January 2001 and is seen here approaching Meadowhall bus station en route to Bradford on the 310 service in May 2007. (K. A. Jenkinson)

Leaving Meadowhall bus station on 27 May 2007 is Dunn Line Caetano-bodied Volvo B12B 0626 (FN06 FKZ), which began life in July 2006 and wears corporate National Express livery with 'Airport' branding. (K. A. Jenkinson)

Sporting branding for route 88, Stagecoach Yorkshire Alexander Dennis-bodied MAN 18.220 22432 (YN07 KRE) heads through Ecclesfield on its way to its depot on 23 May 2007 when only a few weeks old. (K. A. Jenkinson)

Seen on Meadowhall Road, Sheffield, on 23 May 2007 is TM Travel's Plaxton-bodied Mercedes Benz 0814D S582 RGA, which had begun life north of the border with White Ribbon, East Kilbride, in February 1999. (K. A. Jenkinson)

New to Norfolk Green, Kings Lynn, in January 2003, TM Travel Optare Solo MW52 PZD is seen here leaving Meadowhall bus station on the 261 service to Dinnington on 25 May 2007. (K. A. Jenkinson)

Pictured here on 3 June 2009 when only a few weeks old is Sheffield Community Transport Alexander Dennis Enviro200 MX09 MHN. (M. Quinney)

With an advertising panel blocking its passengers' view of Sheffield, First South Yorkshire's Wright-bodied Volvo B7RLE 69056 (SF55 UBS), which had started life with First Glasgow (No. 1) in February 2006, is seen here passing the city's Pond Street bus station on 24 March 2010. (K. A. Jenkinson)

Departing from Pond Street bus interchange on 24 March 2010 on the FreeBee Sheffield city centre service is Wellglade-owned TM Travel Plaxton-bodied MAN 12.240 1199 (YN08 JWD). (K. A. Jenkinson)

Seen in Sheffield's Pond Street bus interchange awaiting its limited stop Chesterfield 727 service passengers in March 2010 is Stagecoach East Midland's twelve-year-old Jonckheere-bodied Volvo B10M 52633 (S673 RWJ). (K. A. Jenkinson)

Painted in Veolia livery, Dunn Line Alexander Dennis Enviro200 YX09 HYY rests in Sheffield Pond Street bus interchange on 24 March 2010 before undertaking its next journey on the A1 service to Rotherham. (K. A. Jenkinson)

Also operating the A1 service to Rotherham on 24 March 2010 is Dunn Line's Veolia-liveried Optare Solo YJ06 YPT, which was new in July 2006. (K. A. Jenkinson)

New to Kentish Bus in February 1990, Wellglade-owned TM Travel Northern Counties dual-door-bodied Leyland Olympian 1107 (G531 VBB) is seen here in Sheffield Pond Street bus interchange on 24 March 2010. (K. A. Jenkinson)

Starting life with Dublin Bus in January 1992 registered 92-D-126, this Alexander (Belfast)-bodied Leyland Olympian was acquired by TM Travel in April 2006, converted from dual- to single-door configuration, and re-registered J628 CEV. Here it is seen in Sheffield bus interchange in April 2010 after TM travel was acquired by Wellglade and given fleet number 1113. (K. A. Jenkinson)

One of a number of Alexander-bodied tri-axle Leyland Olympians purchased by North Anston independent MASS Transit from Kowloon Motor Bus, Hong Kong, in 2003. Seen here in Sheffield in BrightBus livery in April 2010 is C884 RFE, which in Hong Kong was registered DJ3 644. (K. A. Jenkinson)

Seen in Sheffield early in 2009 when only a few months old is TM Travel Optare Solo YN58 NDV. (K. A. Jenkinson)

Purchased new by TM Travel in March 2007 but seen here in Sheffield city centre in March 2010 after its passage to the Wellglade Group, is Plaxton-bodied VDL SB120 1185 (YJ07 JNN). (K. A. Jenkinson)

Heading through Sheffield city centre adorned with route 120 branding on 24 March 2010 is Stagecoach Yorkshire East Lancs-bodied Volvo B6BLE 31912 (LR02 EHH), which was new to Metropolitan Omnibus, North Acton, in April 2002 and then passed via Yorkshire Traction subsidiary Yorkshire Terrier, who converted it from dual- to single-door configuration, before reaching Stagecoach in December 2005. (K. A. Jenkinson)

Carrying branding for the 43 service from Chesterfield to Sheffield, Stagecoach East Midland Alexander Dennis-bodied MAN 18.240 22612 (YN08 JGU) is seen here in Pond Street, Sheffield, in April 2010. (K. A. Jenkinson)

New to Capital Citybus in August 1996, First South Yorkshire Northern Counties-bodied Volvo Olympian 30554 (P243 HMD) is seen here in Sheffield on 24 March 2010 wearing Unibus livery for the 80 service from the city centre to Hallam University. (K. A. Jenkinson)

Looking smart in its operator's 'Barbie (willow leaf)' livery, with the city's railway station in the background, First South Yorkshire Alexander-bodied Volvo B10M 60609 (N777 CKY) approaches Sheffield bus interchange on 24 March 2010. (K. A. Jenkinson)

Starting life in London with First CentreWest in April 1999, First South Yorkshire Northern Counties-bodied Volvo Olympian 34107 (T907 KLF) is pictured here in Sheffield city centre in April 2010. (K. A. Jenkinson)

Heading a line of BrightBus vehicles on school contracts in Sheffield in March 2010 is Northern Counties-bodied Scania N113DRB K863 LMK. A much-travelled bus, it began life with London Buses in September 1992 and then passed to Stagecoach East London, Stagecoach East Kent, and Stagecoach Manchester Magicbus before being acquired by BrightBus. (K. A. Jenkinson)

Seen in Sheffield city centre branded for cross-city route 83 is Stagecoach Yorkshire Alexander Dennis-bodied MAN 18.220 22439 (YN07 KRV). (K. A. Jenkinson)

New to Sheffield City Council in February 2007 is sixteen-seat welfare-bodied Ford Transit 50673 (FH56 XPN), seen here in April 2010 parked on double-yellow lines in the city centre. (K. A. Jenkinson)

New to Mainline in August 2002 and leased to other operators who won the tender to provide a rural links service in the Sheffield area, Optare Solo 1157 (YL02 FKU) is seen here in Pond Street bus interchange in March 2010 with T Travel logos when operated by Wellglade-owned TM Travel. (K. A. Jenkinson)

Seen in Pond Street, Sheffield, on 24 March 2010 is Stagecoach East Midland Optare Excel 35000 (YN51 VHH), which was purchased new in October 2001. (K. A. Jenkinson)

Starting life with First South Yorkshire in September 2008, Wright-bodied Volvo B9TL 37523 (YN58 ETO) is seen here in Sheffield in April 2010 with branding on its upper-deck side windows for routes 75 and 76. (K. A. Jenkinson)

Carrying branding for routes 46/47 below its lower-deck side windows and further generic branding on its upper-deck side and front windows is First South Yorkshire Wright-bodied Volvo B9TL 37482 (YN08 NLZ), caught by the camera in Sheffield in April 2010. (K. A. Jenkinson)

Wearing an all-over white livery without any indication of its operator, except for its legal lettering, is Sheffield Community Transport Optare Solo MX08 MYP, leased from Mistral (dealer) and seen here in Sheffield bus interchange on 24 March 2010. (K. A. Jenkinson)

Wearing Stagecoach's most recent Supertram livery, 106 is seen here in the city centre en route to Herdings Park in April 2010. (K. A. Jenkinson)

New to Mainline, First South Yorkshire Wright-bodied Volvo B10BLE 60657 (T839 MAK) waits for the traffic lights to change in Sheffield city centre on 24 March 2010 alongside Stagecoach Yorkshire Alexander-bodied MAN 18.220 22087 (MX54 LRN), which began life with Stagecoach Manchester. Note the Supertram signs on the post to the right. (K. A. Jenkinson)

Passing through Pond Street bus interchange, Sheffield, after completing a journey from London on the 560 service on 24 March 2010 is National Express Caetano-bodied Scania K340EB4 CO52 (FJ57 KJU), which carries branding on its side windows and lower panels for the London to Stansted Airport service. (K. A. Jenkinson)

Starting life with Yorkshire Traction subsidiary Andrews in March 2000 and passing to Stagecoach with the YTC business five years later, East Lancs-bodied DAF SB220 26101 (W471 MKU) awaits a driver change in Sheffield city centre on 24 March 2010. (K. A. Jenkinson)

New to Sheffield Community Transport in November 2008, UVM-bodied Mercedes Benz 515CDI WR59 AVM is seen here in Sheffield city centre on 24 March 2010 wearing T Travel South Yorkshire and Door2Door logos. (K. A. Jenkinson)

Leaving Meadowhall bus station en route to Sheffield on the 909 service from its home city is Stagecoach Hull Plaxton-bodied Volvo B10M P178 PRH. (K. A. Jenkinson)

On the 253 service to Crystal Peaks is Stagecoach Yorkshire Wright Commander-bodied DAF SB220 26127 (YJ04 HLC), which began life with Rapson, Inverness, in April 2004. (M. Quinney)

New to Capital Citybus, London, in October 1998, after being transferred to First South Yorkshire, Northern Counties-bodied Leyland Olympian 34213 (S213 LLO) is pictured here about to enter Sheffield Pond Street interchange on 24 March 2010. (K. A. Jenkinson)

Wearing First South Yorkshire's new Sheffield livery is Wright Gemini-bodied Volvo B9TL 36275 (BD12 TCO), which was new to First Games Transport in June 2012 for use on the London Olympics shuttles. (Karol Koronowski)

Displaying Stagecoach's new 'local' livery and seen here in Sheffield city centre en route to Batemoor is Alexander Dennis-bodied Scania N230UD 15713 (YN60 CKG), which began life in October 2010. (Kat's Transport Photography)

Caught by the camera running on national railway track between Meadowhall and Rotherham is Stagecoach Tram-Train 299 303. (CAMRA)

Seen here superbly preserved in South Yorkshire Transport's Little Nipper livery is Optare-bodied Dennis Domino 53 (C53HDT), which was new in September 1985. (Tommy Holland)